T0196704

CLEARING UP YOUR CLOSET CHAOS

The Busy Women's Quick Start Guide To Decluttering Your Closet!

MARTHA BROWN JONES

authorHOUSE®

AuthorHouse™
1663 Liberty Drive
Bloomington, IN 47403
www.authorhouse.com
Phone: 833-262-8899

Published by AuthorHouse 04/29/2022

ISBN: 978-1-6655-5833-4 (sc)
ISBN: 978-1-6655-5832-7 (e)

Library of Congress Control Number: 2022907900

Print information available on the last page.

CONTENTS

DISCLAIMER

Please be advised: This book is solely for educational and personal empowerment, and is not intended to be a substitute for professional advice. I am not a licensed/registered decluttering service professional; however, I am qualified to recommend decluttering tips based on the success I've had decluttering my own closet.

Even while juggling life and the busy schedules that come with it, decluttering can be done with ease and speed. Let's dive in the pages, and get you started on your own journey to a decluttered closet!

DEDICATION

This book is dedicated to my Lord and Savior, Jesus Christ. Thank You for keeping me through the storms in my life. Thank You for instilling Your Holy Spirit inside me to hear Your voice giving me direction, guidance, support and unconditional love.

To my loving husband of over 33 years, Anthony A. Jones - "Tony." Whether good or bad, you've navigated this journey with me, and we're both still here. Thank you for your commitment; I love you!

To my only son and encourager, Samuel J. Jones. I love you very much, and I'm so thankful that God has allowed me to see you evolve into the great man of God we prayed for.

To those who encouraged, helped, and prayed me into completing this book, I appreciate you for taking time out of your busy schedules to be there for me in such major ways. You know who you are.

A special thank you to Carol Blackwell for her considerable time and effort in helping me to finalize my book for publishing. Love you sis!

And to my loving mother, the late Inez Celestine Gates Brown (later Pierce after she married), your love made me into the woman I am today. For that, I am grateful. I love and miss you dearly!

"In everything give thanks;
for this is the will of God
in Christ Jesus for you."
1 Thessalonians 5:18

INTRODUCTION

Has your closet ever been bursting with so many different clothes, shoes, purses, hats, scarves and belts that you couldn't find them in there when you needed them? And if you did find what you wanted to wear, how comfortably were you able to put it back where you found it? Did you end up frustrated to the point you decided to get rid of some of the clutter just to breathe again…but maybe found the task harder to accomplish than you thought it would be?

Women love fashion. There's an art to shopping that just makes us feel good! When we look good, we feel good. Matching that favorite top with the perfect skirt or pant and shoes is a euphoric rush of adrenaline that provokes us to buy more clothes than we really need. *Can I get a witness*? Ideally, our closets should be spacious with plenty of breathing room; instead we find ourselves burrowing through all the clutter just to find something to wear, which becomes a whole new chore in itself!

I got my love of clothes from my mother as a young girl many years ago. We couldn't get enough, but because our storage space was limited, we found ourselves constantly purging items to keep our closets organized. When it came to clutter, Mom was no-nonsense; consequently, she passed the importance of living clutter-free on to me. After sadly losing my beloved mother to cancer, organization is a trait that became even more evident in me. It's been my way of keeping her close to my heart.

In 2004, my husband, Tony and I purchased a home with plans to move Mom in with us; however, prior to our plans being fulfilled, she transitioned to her Heavenly home to be with the Lord. After Mom's funeral – in the midst of heart wrenching grief, I was responsible for moving all of her things from the apartment where she lived for 20 years. Cleaning out her one-bedroom apartment (packed with three-bedroom's worth of belongings) was seriously overwhelming, but Mom's gift of organization made the apartment appear to be less crowded than it was. No one would ever have known so many things could fit in such a small space, which made my task easier. As I sorted through her things, deciding where to rehouse them, I remembered Mom telling me that she wanted specific items to be donated to those in need once she was gone. Through the tears, I fulfilled my mother's wishes.

I wanted to share this story with you, because I've come to realize how God has blessed me with the same gift to declutter as He gave to Mom. She graciously passed her talent to minimize onto me, and I'm grateful. I never realized why I enjoy organizing and removing clutter so much until now. Through the years, I've been amazed at how my family and close friends have often complimented my ability to keep things neat, even asking me for help purging and organizing their closets. Yes, you read that right - *closets*!

So, tell me: Is it safe to say that your closets, drawers and storage bins haven't been decluttered in quite a while? Can you admit there's a large portion of your wardrobe that you haven't worn in say, at least two years due to the COVID-19 pandemic, or even prior to it?

In this book, I will teach you effective ways to declutter. Even the busiest women can learn how to annually declutter and keep their spaces organized...including *you*. Alright, without further ado, let's get started!

CHAPTER 1

WHY SHOULD WE DECLUTTER?

What is *clutter*? Clutter is a collection of belongings lying around in an untidy form. Let's face it: we are attached to our belongings. Even though we like them, sometimes we allow them to pile up and get frustrated when they're not easily accessible. This is where the simple solution called **De** (*do the opposite*) **cluttering** comes in. Decluttering means eliminating chaos or disorganization by prioritizing and organizing our possessions, which includes material belongings, commitments, our spiritual state, or anything else pertaining to our well-being. For now, I'll dive into decluttering possessions.

The top three reasons to declutter our closets are:

1. To take inventory of what's inside.
2. To remove unused clothes.
3. To create easy access.

Listen, I found out that some of my girlfriends owned so much *stuff*, they had to jam whatever they could find in an open space all over the house. One of my dearest friends had so many shoes and accessories, she bought a storage house and put it in her backyard instead of renting a unit! It may seem extreme, but it worked for her because it eliminated monthly fees.

God wants us to be good stewards over the possessions He's blessed us with, like our cars and homes. He expects us to maintain what He gives us, keeping everything clean and in order as a show of gratitude for giving them to us. That's why we should keep our things organized and cheerfully give the overflow to someone else who may need it.

Did you know that giving is a form of good stewardship, too? Whether we have an abundance of things we love or a lot scribbled on our wish list, giving away things we no longer use shows appreciation for them. If it's too small, too large or just plain outdated, don't hoard it, bless a woman who can use it instead. Not only will she be excited to have her wardrobe increased, you'll feel lighter and wonderful, too!

"It's time to lose the stuff you don't use!"

CHAPTER 2

THE REALITY OF DECLUTTERING

Another advantage to decluttering is that once the physical "junk" is removed, your mind will be a lot clearer, too.

Many of us believe we don't have enough time to get started. Allow me to prove otherwise. It's not always that we don't have time, it's that we mismanage the time we have. Come out of that mindset. There IS enough time. Keep reading to see how we can do better to cancel the clutter.

Schedule it. Put together a daily schedule of tasks to ease the feeling of anxiety and being overwhelmed. Organizing our day helps alleviate those moments when we feel like we're too busy to have peace. Those "*To do*" lists break down what seems like heavy loads into manageable assignments that allow us to breathe.

Other ways to eliminate the anxiety of decluttering while making the time pass quickly is by playing our favorite music or having a conversation as we work. It turns decluttering from being a burden into fun. When the task is going well and you're feeling accomplished, be creative in rewarding yourself for a job well done. Staying on schedule is a reward within itself, but when the clutter's gone from your house, it feels even better. Especially when it's in the consignment shop, thrift store, or someone else's closet instead of taking up space in yours.

"Every time I purge I get an urge to splurge!"

CHAPTER 3

GETTING STARTED
WITH DECLUTTERING

The number one issue women have when decluttering our closets is the fear of getting rid of something we love by mistake. Allowing anxiety to rush us during the purge can cause us to accidentally get rid of something we intended to keep. Using a systematic method to purge in an organized way can alleviate confusion, and help us keep what we want and get rid of what we don't.

First things first: **DO NOT** pull all of your items out of your closet. You'll end up quitting before you start. Choose a category and pick a day to eliminate what you don't want to keep. If your closet isn't bursting at the seams, you may be able to eliminate two categories per week. Thirty minutes for purging is a good place to start, but you can work longer if time permits.

Systematically organizing our clothing and accessories can be accomplished in as little as two weeks by implementing the one category per day method. *(See sample category chart at end of Chapter 4).* As soon as you complete one category, you can move on to the next. As you progress, moving things around should be easier, because most of the clutter has been eliminated by selling or giving it away along the way.

Keep in mind that you can't measure your success based on someone else's results, as their goals may be different from yours. Our closets are different sizes, and the size of our wardrobes vary; our goals may not be the same, but we can all accomplish something in a thirty-minute window. To successfully achieve your downsizing target, be diligent, keep your goal in mind as you work, move at your own pace, and know that results will vary.

This process doesn't have to be overwhelming *(refer to the motivators and rewards in Chapter 4)*. A systematic approach to making the process smoother is key. Depending on the amount of clothes you have, it can take 30 days or less to minimize or completely eliminate the clutter.

"Look at me working towards being clutter free!"

CHAPTER 4

ENJOYABLE TIPS BEFORE, DURING AND AFTER DECLUTTERING

Here are a few suggestions to motivate or reward yourself for a cleaner closet:

1. Schedule a 30-minute massage.

2. Treat yourself to a pedicure or manicure.

3. Watch a movie you want to see or a good TV show.

4. Listen to an audio book.

5. Have a conversation with a friend.

6. Treat yourself to coffee at Dunkin' Donuts or Starbucks.

7. Soak in the tub with lit candles, dim lights and soothing music while sipping your favorite beverage.

8. Get a facial.

9. Enjoy an ice cream cone.

10. Volunteer for an hour.

11. Learn something new.

12. Journal your thoughts.

13. Create a playlist of all the songs that uplift and bring you joy.

14. Stroll around the block or have a quick workout for 30 minutes.

15. Scroll through photo albums, the camera roll or Google Photos to brighten the day.

"I need incentive to remain attentive."

Sample Chart for Decluttering
CLOTHING/SHOES CATEGORY

TYPE	TOTAL #	SEASON	STYLE	KEEP #	DONATE #	CONSIGN #	Receipt	COMPLETE
Pants	30	Spring	Jeans	14	10	6	✓	✓
Dresses								
Blouses								
Shirts								
Sweaters								
Special Occasional								
Shoes								

Fill chart with categories that fits your closet decluttering need.

CHAPTER 5

SYSTEMATIC
DECLUTTERING
PROCESS

Decluttering Your Closet by Category

Let's dive deeper into how to declutter by category. First, separate your clothes by the category denoted on the chart I provided, then focus on a single category at a time before tackling the next.

Categories can be separated by:

1. Type
2. Color
3. Season

Once grouped together, assess the value of each piece to judge how much they mean to you. From there, decide which pieces you want to keep and remove the unwanted ones. Cluttered closets with no order can be very frustrating, especially when the chaos keeps us from easily grabbing what we want to wear.

In a way, decluttering our closets is like shopping for something new; it can bring many surprises! Before making any new purchases, it's good to take inventory of your wardrobe – that piece you want may already be in your closet.

The results of a decluttered closet are an open space to walk into, and saving money by not buying something you already have. Who wants to waste time digging around looking for a shirt we'll probably never find under all the mess, when we can quickly grab it, throw it on, and go? Save time and money by putting the sample chart to work to decide which items are staying in your home, and those that have to find a new place to live.

"I gave it away, now I have
more space in my closet."

CHAPTER 6

STEPS I USED TO DECLUTTER AND ORGANIZE

At some point during the day, our clothes either go on or come off. After we undress, we toss the clothes where we can easily find them later, especially if they're go-to pieces. Knowing where to find everything is the first step to effectively organizing what we wear on a regular basis, versus what we rarely find ourselves putting on. Let's take a look at the organization plan that helped me along the way.

1. PANTS

Step 1: Sort pants by category. For example, most of us have more than one pair of jeans in different colors and styles, right? How about we start there.

Step 2: Gather all your jeans from your closets, drawers and bins. Put all the ones you don't wear anymore, or haven't worn in a year or longer. Toss the ones that are in bad condition, permanently stained, or torn *(even though in this culture, torn jeans are the fad)*, or the wrong fit.

Step 3: Group the eliminated jeans in a purge pile that you're either keeping or giving away. (Be mindful that the jeans you plan to sell should be in good to excellent condition, wrinkle-free and ready for purchase). Keep the jeans you regularly wear, with a limit of 14 pairs. If you wear jeans every day, then you'd have two weeks' worth to wear, even if you don't wear them 14 days straight.

Step 4: If you have jeans in different colors, repeat the process of keeping and/or eliminating duplicate ones in the category you're concentrating on. Evaluate their condition, size, and whether or not you'll miss them when they're gone. Keep your favorites, being careful not to exceed your limit of 14.

Step 5: Hang or neatly fold the jeans you decide to keep and store them on your closet shelves or in drawers (whichever you prefer), to keep them organized and accessible.

Step 6: Divide the jeans you've decided to toss into the following categories: sell, thrift, or donate. Starting with regular jeans, work your way through capris, denim shorts, rompers, leggings, etc. until every pair has been checked and assigned to their new place.

Step 7: Clean and pack the clothes you're sending to the thrift store, and hang whatever's going to the consignment shop or that you're selling. **Do this each week**. (Keep in mind clean, pressed clothes sell better).

The condition they're given away in also speaks to your level of stewardship.

Please Note: For tax purposes, request a copy of the receipts when you can if you plan to itemize them during tax season. I also suggest taking pictures of what you sell and/or give away to the thrift store in case you're audited later.

2. DRESSES

Now about these dresses! Ladies always have a bevy of dressy dresses, maxi dresses, summer dresses, spring dresses, fall dresses, winter dresses, work dresses, casual dresses, church dresses, cocktail dresses, and gowns for special occasions on hand. There are just so many to choose from, whew!

No matter how many dresses you have and no matter the style, you can still perform the same process of elimination that you used for all those jeans you have. (Or *had* if you've already completed the process). Sort through all your black dresses, and keep the 14 you must *have*. This leaves you with up to two weeks' worth when you're done. You may want to keep more, which is fine as long as you have a closet big enough to store them.

3. BLOUSES

This is a fun one! Pair your long-sleeved blouses from the short-sleeved, then divide them by color and season.

Once again, keep the ones you like, and get rid of the rest. If you don't have a huge number of blouses, you may only need to keep up to five, depending on how much closet space you have. And don't forget to include t-shirts, pullover tees, tank tops and sweaters.

4. SHOES

Some ladies say we can never have too many shoes, but your closet may not agree. Take a deep breath, because you have a ton of shoes to go through: dress shoes (pumps, flats, high heels), boots, sandals, flip-flops, tennis shoes, slippers, etc. Then there are the sub-categories like boots, which can be broken into 3-quarter heels, short heels, long boots and so on. The easiest way to sort your shoes is to work one group at a time. How about we start with the *cute* shoes, you know...the ones that hurt your feet! I call these "*sitting down shoes*", "*see my new cute shoes*", and "*don't ask me to walk fast shoes.*" None of this footwear is comfortable or healthy for our feet, so don't feel bad about giving them away to someone who can stand the pain.

I know shoes are the hardest to part with, but get a trash can and toss those shoes that are worn and have run-down heels right on inside the bin. I'll allow a reprieve if they can be repaired, and you actually plan on taking them to get fixed. However, if they're going to just sit in the closet for another year without fixing them...trash them.

Alright, we're down to sandals. We love a good sandal, but I bet we don't wear all the sandals we have. Do we need

100 pairs of flip flops? Probably not. Just like we broke down the clothes in our closet down by color, size, etc. let's minimize our shoes by doing the same. I understand if you want to keep certain pairs to match specific outfits, but don't use that as an excuse not to clear the ones out that you don't intend on wearing when they're in season. And speaking of season, are you still going to wear that sandal if you're getting rid of the summer clothes that go with them? Keep that in mind as you work.

Now it's time to decide how and where to store your shoes. I suggest keeping the box they come in, then stacking them by type, which makes them easier to find. You can stack them on the shelves in your closet or on the floor below your clothes by pushing them all the way to the wall. Didn't save the shoe boxes? I have the perfect solution - either buy clear shoe tree hangers for the back of your closet, or clear stackable shoe/boot boxes.

Get creative, neatly organize, and remember to return everything back to the space you've designated for it. Following the process minimizes clutter and the headaches that come with it.

Just a Recap: Remember, 30 minutes a day is all you need if you follow the process the same way to navigate through your entire closet. Turn on some music, an audiobook, or your favorite television show, set your focus on a single category at a time, and get to work. You'll be surprised how quickly the time will pass, and how much you'll accomplish while still having fun. Work at your own pace and know that whatever you achieve in that half-hour will be a great accomplishment towards completing the process. Give yourself a few weeks or a month max to transform your closet. It all depends on you. You don't have to be overwhelmed…you can do this!

If you still find yourself overwhelmed by trying to follow the steps, feel free to contact me at <u>Clutterfree105@ gmail.com</u> to book a session via Zoom, FaceTime, or Duo. I'll help you get the hang of it. If you've been able to complete the process using this guide, congratulations - you made it! Everything taking up unnecessary space is out of the house, and I bet you feel physically and mentally lighter. Exhale. Look at what you've accomplished! I'm so, so proud of you!

"Stepping out of the clutter into the decluttered!"

CHAPTER 7

DECLUTTERING YOUR SPIRITUAL LIFE

When we began discussing the process of decluttering, we defined "declutter" as removing mess or disorganization to organize and prioritize. The opposite of clutter, right?

In case you haven't implemented a systematic way to declutter your spiritual life, the process is similar in some ways as organizing and prioritizing your closet. There may be things cluttering your mind and spirit that will make life much better once they're purged. Get rid of dead weight that keeps you from moving forward. *Worry...* dead weight. *Frustration...*dead weight. *Fear...*dead weight. *Sin...*dead weight. The process of decluttering the spirit isn't done alone. God's Holy Spirit is here to help you get it done!

Here are two important questions:

1. If you died today, are you certain you'll make it into Heaven?
2. When you die and stand before God, how will you respond when He asks, "Why should I let you into My Heaven?"

There is only one answer.

I have five foundational truths to share with you:

Foundational Truth #1

God is good, and He is a God of love who does not want anyone to perish.

John 3:16 NKJV-

> "For God so loved the world that He gave His only begotten Son, that whoever believes in Him should not perish but have everlasting life."

Foundational Truth #2

All men are sinners, and sin separates us from God.

Romans 3:23 NKJV-

> "For all have sinned and fall short of the glory of God."

Foundational Truth #3

The penalty for man's sin is death.

Romans 6:23 NKJV-

> "For the wages of sin is death, but the gift of God is eternal life in Christ Jesus our Lord."

Foundational Truth#4

Calvary is God's only provision for man's sin.

Romans 5:8NKJV-

> "But God demonstrates His love toward us, in that while we were still sinners, Christ died for us."

Foundational Truth #5

Our responsibility is to exercise saving faith. Saving faith is claiming by personal choice and relying completely upon Christ's work on The Cross to be sufficient payment for our sins.

John 6:47 NKJV-

> "Most assuredly, I say to you, He who believes in Me (Jesus) has everlasting life."

Romans 10:9 NKJV-

> "That if you confess with your mouth the Lord Jesus and believe in your heart that God has raised Him from the dead, you will be saved."

Now that I've armed you with scriptures to strengthen your spiritual foundation, what's preventing you from trusting in Jesus Christ and His shed blood to receive Him as your Lord and Savior? If you realize there's nothing holding you back and you've decided to surrender your cluttered life to Jesus Christ, please contact me; I will be happy to help you understand more about this beautiful journey.

Email: Clutterfree105@gmail.com

(Some information from Chapter 7 is shared from *Moody Press*, a division of Moody Bible Institute designed for education, evangelization, and edification. Moody Press c/o MLM, Chicago, Illinois 60610).

Printed in the United States
by Baker & Taylor Publisher Services